Tiny Footcrunch

David Wasserman

Published by Unsolicited Press

www.unsolicitedpress.com

Copyright © 2018 David Wasserman

All Rights Reserved.

Unsolicited Press Books are distributed to the trade by Ingram.

ISBN: 978-1-947021-26-6

Cover Design: In-house UP team

Attention schools and businesses. Discount copies are available for bulk orders. Please contact our team at info@unsolicitedpress.com.

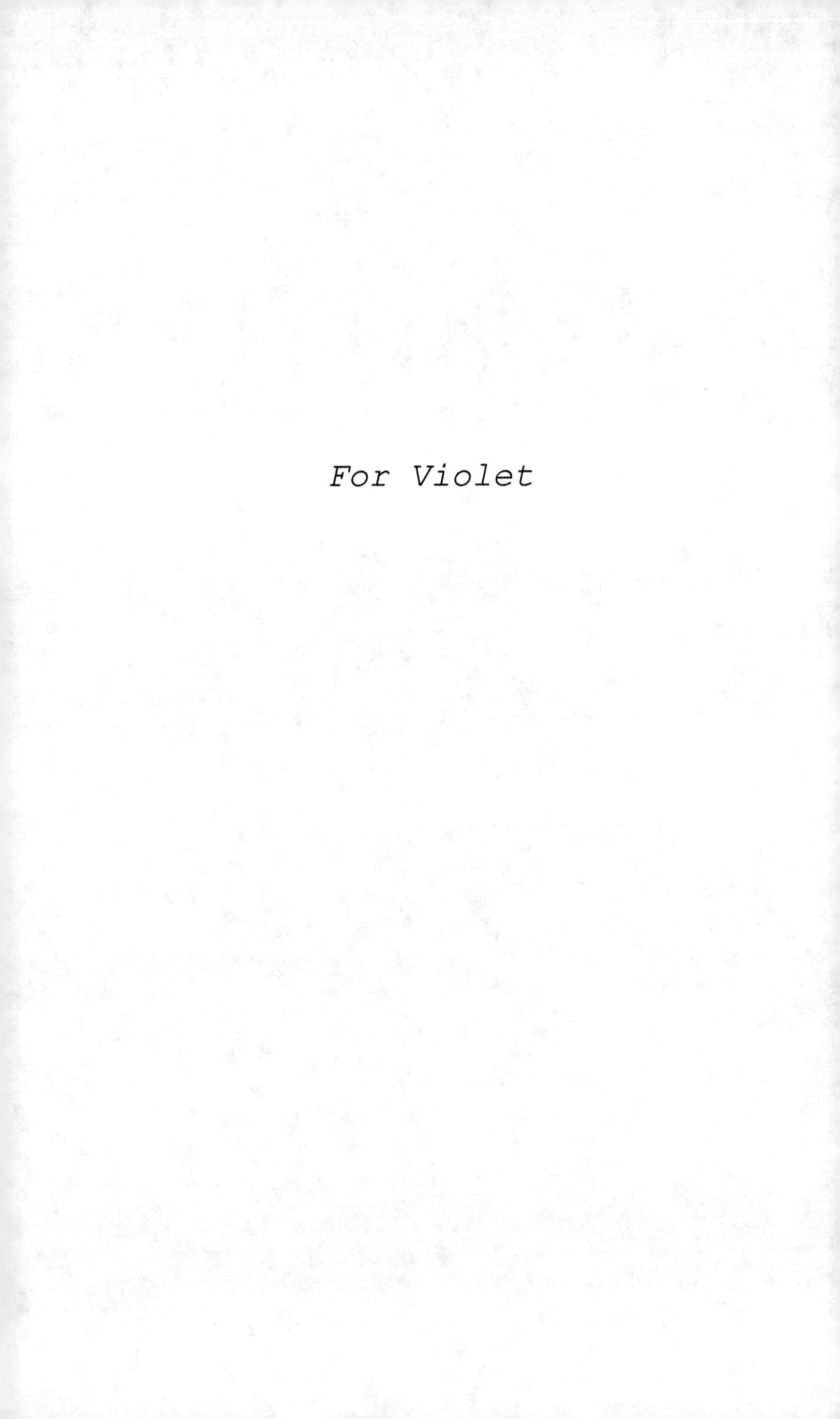

For Violet

Contents

<u>Preface</u>

My reading had abated - replaced by Twitter, Facebook and text messages. Loyal bedtime and travel companions forever migrated. Needing a portal back, I reunited with poetry. Short poems. Haiku. Senryu. Monoku. Pops. These felt more familiar and approachable now than ever before - kissing cousins to the texts, tweets and posts I (most of society?) had been reading.

That's how this book was born. Not red and screaming into this world but rather quiet - wind wisp whisper whimpers turned cries turned first words.

Keep it on your nightstand. Toss it in your bag. Get yourself back to literature with this chapbook gateway drug. This key.

You might find one poem (one line even!) you keep going back to without a conscience reason. Over and over it builds as if a mantra

circle train on a track - chugga
chugga chugga chugga around and
around your head until it either
slows with a peaceful gush of air
or crashes - boom! into one bright
moment of understanding.

ball lightning

a certain line

lingers in my mind

<u>Sadness</u>

Tiny footcrunch
Don't!
Fresh snow

first babysitter
dinner fork
in the road

Thanksgiving argument -
wish I could go back
four seconds

a piece of paper
in the back bedroom trash bin
list of baby names

where did you go?
smudges on the window

vanilla overtures
inevitably
fade

empty bird feeders
and houses
forever migrated

Italian woman
seasoned by
onion tears

annoying -
a stubborn splinter
from an immature coffin

second grade math class
decomposing numbers
and a student's parent

<u>Joy</u>

the sweaty child
is more affectionate
    -      I cringe

smiling, I watch
you gasp
in my words

baby whale
first breath -
green glass water

                    open ocean
              half-buried chair
                 the same blue

          childhood house
          the neighbor's cat
          tree still standing

february march
newborn fish
hooked

second date
county fair food stand
a little hay in the roll

          you are the sole
          architect of
          your soul

                              cupped hands
                              coypu hunter
                              sips stars

          caressing your spine
          smelling your
          chapters

<u>Anger</u>

I would be mad, too.
Little white hornet rebuilds
again and again

Cowardly plant!
Bows its head
when dying

sunsets are so easy for you

                         tears and thunder
              rolled down the landscape
                           of her face

              Spring equality -
              all this green and
              those little pink flowers

Second Amendment
shooting the breeze
silent funeral

rhinoceros dreams
tear down
a horn gate

         clipped words
          and nails
      crescent moon tonight

                    April again . . .
                      your anger
                       rained in

   a roadkilled squirrel smiles
     it's cousin   dashes
             in fr-

<u>Kindness</u>

conifer branch reaches
to a naked neighbor

                    winking squares
                    callused leather
                    cherry tree smile

                              partridge days
                              I forgive you
                              drummer days

12

homeless
snow falls
new blanket

watering can hose off summer stains

snowdrops . . .
I cover
my wife's cold shoulder

crepuscular rays
I listen to my partner's
perspective tonight

            hair clippings
        scattered among the floor
            in solidarity

                monochrome rainbow
                scattered colors I
                invite inside

        old colorblind mare –
        races don't matter
        to her

<u>Fear</u>

15

a noise
in the dark
my light shifting

no one spared -
bowling alley
shooting

odd creaking
of a house
old bones

                          uncomfortable
                       on the ground,
                     a robin hops . . .

                    hatred
                 flickering orange
              . . . August advances

      shiftly passing
      a blue gown
      I hear a bell

lifting
the dark
ordinary

                now penniless
            a distraught child
        learns about the train crash

                        maybe the baby
                        won't like me
                            either

        squirrels chattering
            teeth biting
        winter wind

<u>Love</u>

I will love you
if the world ends
and if it doesn't

        seeing you
        watching the
        falling rain

        wildflower bed . . .
            the Earth tilted
        toward you and me

a love poem
in the middle of
my honey-do list

whoosh whoosh
my heartbeat catching up

black and white picture
wide eyes gazing at
a growing violet

you can do better
breathed softly to me
ignoring alarms

                not much said -
           November walk around
            the deep reservoir

                        our fingers
                    slightly heavier
                          forever

           mistrain morning
              air thick
            with our love

                  20

<u>Confusion</u>

sun mask sand shoes wind clothes
a child has drowned

restless sleep: who WHO who WHO who WHO?

                              feline eyes
                      could see through
                         this darkness

post-storm morning
drowned cicadas
terracotta suicide

silent nursery
the crying and dying
of plants

waking up this morning
not morning
somewhere else

an eagle's cry -
her screams
were also piercing

    this is the last time
    we'll be tortured again

                 contagious -
                    I yawn
                 your yawn

    offensive ballplayer
      crosses
      the line

Humor

ice tipped mountains -
beautiful!
how much?
that's mean!

                    I'm pregnant!

            -       pause

                        window feelings
                -       blindsided

                    focused intently
          on this one single moment
              oh look, a Snapchat!

            depressed
            basketball
              sharp
             shooter

piles of candy
a plastic pumpkin
Reformation Day

as if
enlightened

          golf   is
                    playing   fetch
     with   yourself

                         animal cruelty
                          the elephant
                          in the room

               speed dating
               selective
               mute

<u>Curiosity</u>

snowbirds
visiting the palm
readers

            cat's head
        between spindles
        fall or spring?

                        a wind chimes
                    in whichever key
                        we make it

                    hades hydrangea,
                     glacier blue -
                  three prefer hiding

          rifling through
          my grandfather's
          old war chest

loving words
tender embraces
still . . .

baseball field in November
bats begin to
hibernate

          blooms buried
          in Gordon Square
          writer's block

                    opening up -
               I set the burner
                    to simmer

          still life . . .
          wanting more than
          these apples and pears

<u>Hope</u>

dead geranium -
so good to see you again!

                    Dustoff!
              eyeward and lifted
              dandelion field

                    I did not find you
              when I searched the world
                            this time

my breath
the dying Earth
a tree's breath

infant hands
catch a wind
red sky

nightingale gold
spattered rivers
for a song

neapolitan
spilled and mopped
at a poor parlor

                grocery ghost
                cleared for takeoff
                summer in the city

        bravely asking ... the wind...

                wormy moon
                stars melt
                the snow

About the Author

David Wasserman currently teaches second grade and lives in the mostly quiet woods of Connecticut with  his wife and daughter. Poetry had been calling to him through the growing noise of texts tweets beeps buzzing ringing - and finally got through in its own tiny way.

Tiny Footcrunch is David's first book.

About the Press

34

UNSOLICITED PRESS is a small publishing house based in the Pacific Northwest. You can learn more at www.unsolicitedpress.com.